Reporters Are Looking For You!

Get the Publicity You Need to Build Your Business

By Dan Janal

Reporters Are Looking For You!
Reporters Need You
It's a Fact

Introduction

Hundreds of reporters, each and every day, post queries hoping to find experts and sources for their articles. These reporters work for every publication from the New York Times to local newspapers and national magazines.

But the competition among experts and sources for those leads has grown as well. More people than ever are responding to reporters – but aren't getting quoted because they don't know how to respond effectively. They don't know what to write. They don't know how to write it. And they waste a lot of time wondering how to go about it. Consequently, they don't get quoted and are frustrated.

Since 2001, when I started the PR LEADS service, I've helped thousands of people receive literally millions of dollars of publicity in nearly every major media in the United States.

PR LEADS is the fastest, easiest and most cost-efficient way for authors, speakers, consultants, coaches and small businesses to get publicity.

I've had some clients stick with the service for 7, 8 or even 9 years, which is unheard of in modern marketing.

I've learned a thing or two (or several hundred) ways to get the most publicity possible when working with reporters who are pitching their stories and looking for experts.

This book can help you respond more effectively to reporters so you get more successful pitches and more ink, manage your time more efficiently so you aren't wasting your most important asset – time, and maximize the publicity you do receive.

This short, easy to read e-book contains the essential wisdom to respond to leads quickly and easily so you can get the most out of pitching reporters so you get the publicity you need to become the go-to expert in your industry, and get the publicity you need to build your business.

There are three easy ways to get more publicity right now:

Read it.

Act on it.

Tell me about it.

Good luck!

Table of Contents

Table of Contents

Reporters Are Looking for You!

Overview of PR LEADS

PR LEADS has helped thousands of individual experts, authors, coaches, consultants and small businesses get publicity in nearly every major newspapers and magazine in America.

Founded in 2001 by Dan Janal, PR LEADS ushered in the era of individuals doing their own publicity. It is the only publicity leads service that offers hands-on training and support to help clients learn to work effectively with reporters.

"Publicity is not rocket science. Anyone can get publicity if they have the right tools," says Dan who has more than 30 years of PR experience and was on the PR team that launched AOL.

PR LEADS is based on the ProfNet system from PR Newswire. ProfNet gathers the leads, edits them and sends them to PR LEADS clients. ProfNet also maintains the computer system that lets PR LEADS clients update their own topics and set the schedule to receive leads, all of which are industry firsts and a boon to customer convenience.

PR LEADS adds value by offering free training and support services. All clients get a 90-day training system, access to Dan Janal via conference calls where they can ask any question about the service or publicity. They can also send an unlimited number of responses to Dan for his personal review and feedback so they can get off to a strong start.

"One small coaching tip can lead to a bigger success rate that turns into more publicity for you," said Dan, who has written six books and who has spoken at conferences all around the world – from Beijing to Budapest.

PR LEADS is sold on a monthly subscription basis for $99. To order, go to http://www.PRLEADS.com

Section 1: Getting Reporters to Quote You

This section is divided into four topics:

- What to write in your message so you get your points across clearly and reporters are more likely to use your content and quote you accurately.

- How to think like a reporter so you know what information to provide and how to position yourself so you get the most out of each story.

- How to format your message so it is easy to read and to understand.

- Decide which messages to respond to so you stand the best chance of being quoted.

- Technical how to's for the ProfNet system.

1.   The Million-Dollar Response Template

Here are instructions for responding to leads from reporters. This formula has literally created millions of dollars of publicity for my clients.

Remember, they don't want YOU to write the story. That's their job. They are looking for:
1. Experts
2. Who have something interesting or different to say and
3. Are available NOW!

Your message to them should contain those three elements with the following key components.

First section

Introduce yourself - state your name, book title (if you are an author), or company/business name and position/title (e.g. CEO, sales manager) if you are a businessperson. List 3 places you've been interviewed in national media if you have them, or list 3 top clients or 3 key credentials if you are a consultant. Keep this paragraph to 3-4 sentences. They don't want to read your entire bio. They just need to know who you are. Keep it short!

Second Section

Now offer 2-3 tips that are 2-3 sentences long. Use a separate paragraph for each tip so they are easy to read. Reporters won't use more than 3 sentences, so you stand a better chance of getting quoted if you give them exactly what they need. Write these tips so they are fully contained. In other words, reporters should be able to copy your tips into their articles. This happens all the time!

Third Section

This contains your contact info. Print your name, phone number, e-mail address and website at the minimum. See my contact on the following pages as an example.

Below is a sample ending for a message to reporters, including contact information.

All the best,
Dan

Dan Janal
Publicity Consultant and Publicity Speaker
PR LEADS PLUS Expert Resource Network
dan@prleads.com
http://www.PRLEADSPLUS.com
952-380-1554

I work with speakers, authors, coaches, consultants and small businesses who want to get publicity so they can sell more products and services.

2.   The Magic Formula

Remember the saying, "If you have a hammer, the whole world is a nail?" Let me explain how this can help you get publicity -- and save time.

Whatever your topic is -- the answer to the reporter is YOUR TOPIC. Let's see the answers from one expert who wrote a book about the evils of sugar.

We might not get a lead about sugar, but she can reply to reporters who are writing about:

        Back pain -- sugar causes back pain
        Infertility -- sugar affects body functions
        Bad economy -- sugar imports are affecting this somehow

I might be stretching it here, but the idea is that whatever their problem (within reason), your standard answer about the evils of sugar, or mold, or the benefits of Pilates or hula-hoops will help the reporter.

Think about your hammer and see if you can create one standard response that you can use for a variety of leads, or just to send when you don't have time to be creative!

3.   Get Feedback and Support from Dan Janal

I'm happy to help you improve your responses. Please copy me on your messages, so I see exactly what reporters see. Use this address in the CC or BCC line: dan@prleads.com

4.   Manage Your Time

VITALLY IMPORTANT: It shouldn't take you more than 10 minutes to respond to any message. Manage your time and you will be able to respond to leads quickly and efficiently.

If you don't, you'll feel buried alive.

You'll see other tips about managing your time in the next section of the book. I wanted to underscore this point early on so you can't possibly miss it.

Managing your time is essential to avoiding burnout.

5.   How the Press Decides What to Write About

The New York Times opened their cloak on how stories are created in an article on May 7, 2006 on page 12 of the Week in Review Section. Public Editor Byron Calame reviewed the newspaper on April 16 and asked the reporters and department heads how 23 stories were created. The results will surprise you.

Only 2 of the stories started with PR people. The rest came from ideas from reporters or editors.

What does this mean for authors and experts? The report shows what I've long believed.

Reporters create their own stories and then need to find experts to give the story depth and balance. They need experts. Being in the right place at the right time is an age-old adage. Knowing where to stand, that's why you need to position yourself as an expert.

6. What Do Reporters Look For In A Great Source?

Here's an excerpt from a lead I received from a reporter:

"We're looking for women between the ages of 35 to late 50s who suffered for years from the following: 1) celiac disease; 2) lupus; or 3) mold in her home (the more debilitating her condition, the better the story) and today is in good health."

Notice her words "the more debilitating her condition, the better the story."

That should tell you something. Just in case you were wondering, this person is writing for a major women's magazine, not the National Enquirer!

Do you want to get into the papers?

Be dramatic!

7.   Don't Pitch Off Topic

Obviously, don't respond to any lead that you can't provide tips or opinions. It isn't a good use of your time to pitch reporters on another topic. In fact, they could blackball you if you do.

If the reporter wants to speak to a person who is an expert on fencing and you write, "I don't know anything about fencing, but if you ever need an expert on volleyball, please contact me."

That would be a waste of your time. It would infuriate the reporter and it could get you blackballed from the service.

8.　　Be Bold

Sometimes you honestly disagree with a reporter's premise. That's great! Go contrarian.

Reporters actually want to write stories that show all sides of the picture. So if you see a lead where you think reporters are barking up the wrong tree, don't be afraid to tell them!

That's what makes you an expert!

That's what makes you an individual!

That's what makes you unique and quotable!

Go for it.

9.   Should I respond to all questions?

Sometimes, reporters ask a lot of questions in their queries, or when they call you on the phone.

You do NOT have to answer each question. In fact, I'd suggest you pick only the best question that helps you the most and answer that.

Why?

1. They aren't going to quote you on six answers. They want to quote six different people. So if you have only one shot at the brass ring, grab that ring and forget the others.

2. Also, if you aren't an expert in the other areas, then you'll drag yourself down in their eyes by giving trite answers.

3. Finally, save yourself the time. Managing your time is very important so you don't get overwhelmed. Stay fresh and alert for your next opportunity!

The reporter will get enough responses from other people for the other questions, no worries!

10. Positioning

How will reporters refer to you?

If you tell them you are a doctor, author and speaker, then they will pick one of the three. If you give them one option, they'll have only one choice.

Determine what you want from each article, and position yourself for that outcome.

11.   Positioning for Authors of Multiple Books

As your new book comes out, you will want to promote that instead of the first book.

If you mention the titles of both books, they'll say you are "author of several books" and they might not have enough room to print either title. No one will know the name of either one!

Instead, say you are the author of "THIS BOOK." That way, people will be enticed by your great title and they might want to check it out for more information and possibly, buy it.

I know that this is like saying you are the parent of two children and you mention only one. This is the time for marketing, not boasting!

12.   Don't write the article

Many people write too much information.

This is bad for several reasons:

1. Reporters won't use it all.

2. Reporters will use 1-2 tips at most from one source. They like to quote a variety of people in the article so the reader has a variety of views and opinions.

3. Reporters will use 1-2 sentences from one source. Long answers are hard to read, hard to understand and very hard to edit down to 1-2 sentences. Make it easy on reporters and give them good material in a format they can use.

You spend too much time for not enough return.

Remember, it is the reporter's job to write the article, not yours!

I know that some people respond with messages that are longer than the final article. That's not a good use of your time, or the reporter's time.

13.   Customize Your Response for Each Lead

If you are an expert in five areas, you should mention only the one area that the reporter is looking for. That way you'll look like you are the right fit.

If you are an attorney who can handle matters in 12 areas, then 11 of those are irrelevant to the reporter. If she wants an adoption attorney, tell her that's what you do. Drop the references to family law or other areas that you practice. You'll seem like the perfect fit.

14.   Write exactly what you want quoted

Your tips or ideas should be written exactly as you'd like to see them appear in print.

If the reporter doesn't have time to call you, she could use the material you presented as is.

You'd be surprised how many times reporters will take exactly what you give them and not change a word. That's because they are under deadline pressure and they have to finish the story fast.

15. Offer Steak, Not Sizzle

Sales copy offers lots of sizzle. For example, "Find out how to save hundreds on your next car. Read page 42 of my new book."

That's okay for sales copy, but it is not a good response for reporters.

It would be better to write:

"Save hundreds of dollars on your new car by researching the price of the car on Edmunds.com."

You might think that the first choice would inspire the reporter to call you for more info. The truth is that reporters don't have time to call many sources. If you give them exactly what they need, there's a good chance they will copy your information from your message and paste it into their article.

Remember, you can get quoted without being interviewed. The goal is to get quoted. If you can accomplish this by sending an email, that's great. If a reporter wants to call you for additional information, that's fine, too. But many times, reporters will use the email tips and write the story without talking to you.

16.   Don't Quote Other Experts or Sources

Don't quote other sources. They'll get quoted; you won't.

That includes books, articles and surveys.

If you aren't the expert, then don't respond.

If you think reporters will remember who you are and give you brownie points, you are mistaken. They won't remember who you are five minutes after they read your message.

17.   Stand Out from the Crowd

The best way to stand out from the crowd is to offer unique insights.

Let's face it. Everyone has similar credentials. We've all been to college, consulted with cool companies, written books and won awards. Reporters have seen it all. Our credentials merely make us good candidates to be quoted.

What makes you stand out is your perspective on their story. Our view will be shaped by our experiences.

Draw on those experiences to make yourself stand out from the crowd.

18.   Take Advantage of Your Location

If you see a lead from your local publication, let the reporter know immediately that you are a local resource. Reporters want to feature local people and businesses. All things being equal, you will get the interview over another qualified person if you use this tip.

Your response could start this way:

I'm a dentist working in St. Paul. I have three tips for helping parents get their young children to brush their teeth regularly.

Here are the tips:
1. Tip 1

2. Tip 2

3. Tip 3

If you do this, you'll leapfrog past out-of-town sources.

19. Write Using the First Person

Write in the FIRST person, not the THIRD person.

Example of First Person: I have worked with many major corporations, including American Express, IBM and The Reader's Digest.

Example of Third Person: Mr. Janal has worked with many major corporations, including American Express, IBM and The Reader's Digest.

The first sounds more personal and direct. The second sounds like it came from an official bio or a PR person.

While you might think it sounds classy to have a PR person represent you, the truth is that reporters would much rather deal directly with the expert since it is faster to contact you directly than to deal with an intermediary.

20.   Make Your Message Skimmable

Write for skimming

Reporters get many responses to each lead. They are totally overwhelmed, so they skim. If they see something interesting, they'll stop to read. So your job is to write for skimming.

How can you do that?
1. Use short sentences.

2. Use short paragraphs.

This book is written to be skimmed. Go back and notice my use of lists, bullets, short paragraphs and white space.

21.   Use White Space to Improve Readability

There's nothing harder to read than a dense block of text. That's why newspapers use short sentences and short paragraphs. They'll even start a new paragraph just to open up white space to make the story easier to read. As I demonstrate below. If you do this, reporters will have an easier time reading your notes. I suggest you start a new paragraph each time you start a new thought or tip.

So, put your bio in one paragraph.

Start a new paragraph and put your first tip there.

And so on.

Doesn't the first paragraph look hard to read? That's because it has so many words and so little white space.

Doesn't the rest of the page look so much easier to read?

That's because sentences are short. Paragraphs are short. And white space separates each new thought.

22.   Contact Info

Put your contact info at the end of message and make it look like mine:

All the best,
Dan

Dan Janal
President
PR LEADS PLUS Expert Resource Network
dan@prleads.com
http://www.PRLEADSPLUS.com
952-380-1554

Notice the format:
- Name
- Title
- Company
- Email
- Website
- Phone

23.   How Can My Message Stand Out?
When Sending to a Reporter's Email Account?

Reporters get many responses to their leads and they also get all the spam that you and I receive.

To make your message stand out in their email box, use the reporter's headline as your subject line.

If a reporter wrote: Five ways to beat stress.

You would write: Five ways to beat stress.

24.   Use Lists to Make Each Tip Stand Out

Put each new idea in a separate bullet or a numbered list.

1. Lists are easier to read than long paragraphs

2. It is easier for a report to copy and paste a tip from a list.

3. It is easy for you think concisely if you use lists.

25.   Avoid Hype

When you respond to a query, it should not read like an advertising flyer. It's absolutely deadly to use puff or "hype."

The very words that can be oh-so-very-effective in advertising copy can destroy your chances of gaining a journalist's respect in your news release. Don't try to impress a decision-maker with words like "incredible," "unbelievable," "remarkable," "spectacular, "or "stunning." Words like those have no place in a response. They damage your credibility as a news source. In general, adjectives should be used sparingly.

Definitely avoid any description that sounds "pitchy." Even words like "deluxe" and "easily" can raise red flags with most journalists.

Similarly, stay away from superlatives. Unless you have unbiased research and reliable statistics to back up your claims, stay away from words like "latest," "greatest," "best," etc.

Reporters will go out of their way to prove that your product isn't the latest, greatest or best.

26.   Don't Use All Capital Letters

Some spam filters are beginning to flag messages with all capitals in the subject line. So when you respond to reporters, remember to write the subject line in Upper and Lower Case, like this:

Right: ProfNet: How to lower cholesterol.

Wrong: PROFNET: HOW TO LOWER CHOLESTEROL.

27.   Use Your Spell Checker

No one can proofread his or her own materials effectively, including me.

Fortunately, most email programs have spell checkers, but you MUST turn them on for them to work.

Nothing is more embarrassing than having a typo in a message to a reporter. It could be the kiss of death. You could ruin your credibility with one little typo!

Typos are so easy to prevent – if you turn on your spell checker!

And it doesn't hurt to re-read your messages, either. Don't rely entirely on spell checkers, as they don't catch words that are misused, but spell correctly (i.e. "life" for "live").

28.   Sending Email from ProfNet's system

You can reply to reporters two ways: via your own email account, or via ProfNet's online interface.
I'd suggest you use your own email account. Here's why:

1. You can write more. ProfNet has a word limit.

2. You can include live links to your website. ProfNet can't.

3. You can add formatting cues, like line breaks and paragraphs. ProfNet can't.

Of course, you still might decide to use ProfNet's inbox, and you must use it for leads that are listed as "cloaked."

When you send a note via the ProfNet inbox, you will receive a copy in your regular email box.

29.   Cloaked Queries

From time to time, you might see a lead that is a "cloaked query."

What this means is that the reporter didn't want his or her name and email info available to the general public. You'll see the topic of the query so you can see if it interests you. If it does, then you'll be asked to click on that link to respond to the reporter.

Here is the link in case you need it in the future. https://profnet.prnewswire.com/CommunicationProfessional.asp

You will then sign in to your account. If you've forgotten your username, contact susan@prleads.com. If you've forgotten your password, you can get a new one by clicking the link that says "forgot password."

After you enter your information, such as: joesmith@prleads.com:

- You'll see your inbox, which will contain all the leads in your account, including the cloaked query.

- Locate the query and click on it.

- You will then see a new email box form. Write your answer there. You can write about 400 words.

- Click on "respond to originator" and your message will be sent to the reporter. You'll receive a copy in your email box as well.

30.   Use Twitter to Find More Leads

Reporters who are on tight deadlines can reach you faster if you use Twitter. Instead of waiting for your regular leads which come at a set time(s) each day, you'll be notified immediately when a reporter has a short deadline.

Here's how you can get these special leads via Twitter.

1. You have to register on Twitter (it's free).

2. Go to http://www.twitter.com/profnet

3. Click on the "Follow" button. That's it.

ProfNet posts short-lead requests on Twitter, so it is a good idea to sign up.

Please note: Not all leads are sent via Twitter, only the ones with very short deadlines, as requested by reporters.

31.   Don't harvest reporter's names and email addresses

This is a no-no.

ProfNet and PR LEADS will actually ban you from the service if a reporter notifies them about inappropriate pitching or spamming!

Everyone hates spam and reporters hate inappropriate pitches as much. While you think it might be a good idea to keep track of reporters' names and email addresses, they will actually hate you for it.

Pitch on topic, when needed and you'll be a valuable source for them. There are other, legitimate ways of contacting reporters. If you need a database of reporters go to www.BullsEyePublicity.com.

This service has names and email addresses of reporters who do want to be contacted for relevant pitches from you.

Section 2: Managing Your Time Efficiently

The number one reason why people stop responding to leads is because they feel they don't have enough time. This section will show you how to manage your time effectively so you can respond to more leads efficiently and get more publicity.

This section is comprised of three topics:

1. Manage your time.

2. Manage your topics.

3. Manage your image.

32.   Manage Your Time

You can easily kill a morning responding to one lead. That is a bad use of your time. Why?

Reporters will use 2-3 sentences from you. It shouldn't take you 3 hours to come up with those tips.

You're an expert. You should know the answer off the top of your head.

Give them that answer.

It's probably the best answer!

33.　Set a Time Limit

Set a timer for 10 minutes. That's all the time it should take to respond to any lead.

I'm a fast writer, so I can knock out a response in five minutes or less.

You might need 10 minutes. You might need 15 minutes. Whatever time it is, set a limit and stick to it.

Otherwise, you might spend more time than needed to respond and you will kill your time management system.

Remember, responding to leads should be easy. Don't make it more difficult.

34.　Is there a time of day when you are more productive?

Some of my clients like to respond to leads immediately as they come in. Others like to get one download a day and respond en masse. There is no "best" way for everyone. There is only the best way for YOU. I suggest you try out several options for responding.

Option 1:
> Answer leads as they arrive. Some people can handle the flow. Others can't. Find out what is best for you.

Option 2:
> Answer them at pre-determined times. You can set the delivery schedule to every hour, 2 hours, 4 hours or once a day. See which schedule fits you best.

ProfNet and PR LEADS let you see leads in real time if you visit your online account.

35.   Respond Quickly

The early bird gets the worm.

Working on your schedule is important, but it must be weighed against responding quickly. Some reporters are under a tight deadline and will use the first good messages they get.

If you can, respond quickly.

36.   Don't Follow Up!

Hard as it is to believe, if you don't hear from reporters, assume they are not interested.

Do not send them a follow-up note asking if they are going to use your material, or if they want to arrange an interview. They won't respond.

Reporters get way more good responses than they can use and they simply won't remember the emails from people whose messages they don't use.

Don't waste your time contacting reporters again. Just wait for the next lead to come and respond quickly.

37.   Don't Talk Yourself Out of Answering a Lead

Some people turn down the chance to respond to a lead because they think there is someone who is more qualified.

Don't let this happen to you!

Of course, there is someone who is more qualified. But that person might not ever see the lead. The reporter will work with the person who has the right answer at the right time.

I've seen too many people miss golden opportunities because they didn't believe in themselves.

Don't let this happen to you!

38.   Manage Your Categories and Topics

Don't waste your time receiving or reviewing leads outside your main area of interest. I find that many new clients want to get as many topics and leads as possible. But, after a few days, they realize they really don't want to get leads in all those areas. They want to focus.

ProfNet and PR LEADS always allow clients to decide which topics to get leads from. You can change topics or add topics at any time via your user dashboard or send requests to susan@prleads.com.

39.   Update Your Topic Settings Every 3 Months

Your interests may change over time, so it is a good idea to review your topics and see if there are topics that now apply to you – or if you've moved away from other topics.

Also, as the world changes, new topics come into play, for example corporate social responsibility or learning disabilities.

40.   Were New Topics Added?

Check to see if new categories have been added. You might be pleasantly surprised to find they have added a new category that meets your needs more effectively than an older, broader topic.

You can see topics listed on your account dashboard on the ProfNet system.

41.   Suggest New Topics

You are on the front lines of your industry and see changes and trends before anyone else at a leads provider company. It is in your best interest to suggest new topics to add.

ProfNet has added several dozen new topics over the years to meet the needs of their customers.

To suggest new topics, send an email to susan@prleads.com.

42.   Working with interns and Virtual Assistants

Some people like to have their interns or virtual assistants read leads first and send the best ones to you. This can work, but I've seen it fail so many times. That's because no one knows your topic as well as you do.

You might see an angle in a lead that another person wouldn't see. I've seen this happen many, many times. You could miss important opportunities if your assistant doesn't have your knowledge.

There's no denying this tactic should work and should save you time. However, in order for it to work effectively, you must train that person properly so you get every lead possible.

I'd suggest these steps:

- Show them how to do the work, step by step. Read each lead and show them why it relevant to you or isn't relevant.

- Do this for a few days.

- Let them review the leads with you looking over their shoulder. If they throw away good leads, explain why you think it is a good lead.

- Monitor the process from time to time. Remember, no one knows your business like you do!

43.   Don't Let Assistants Respond to Leads for You

There's no way assistant can respond the way you can. I've seen many people try this and only one has had any degree of success.

At best, a surrogate can send your resume to a reporter. But this won't set you apart from dozens (or hundreds) of other experts who are responding with real tips, facts and ideas. It would be a waste of time.

44.   Managing Expectations

You don't get hired for every speaking engagement even though you think you are perfect. You don't sell your book to every publisher even though you think it is perfect. You don't get hired for every job even though you think you are perfect. The same is true with publicity leads. You won't get interviewed for every article even though you think you are perfect.

Our clients generally get interviewed 1 time for every 10 messages they respond to. That's a 10 percent success rate, which in marketing is absolutely fantastic! Most direct mail marketers are thrilled to get a 2 percent response. With PR LEADS, you might get a response rate that is 5 times better than an expensive direct mail campaign. Human nature being what it is, it is only natural to feel dejected if reporters don't contact you for every message. But let's agree, that is unrealistic. If you get 1 in 10 you are doing well - and you'll have more PR than you'll know what to do with over the course of a year!

45.   Scan Leads

If you have time to read the newspaper in the morning, you have time to respond to leads.

It's really the same process.

You read 2-3 articles. You scan a few others and you throw the rest of the paper out without even opening some sections (like classifieds, or sports or world news). Yet, you feel like you got your money's worth.

It's the same with queries. You skim the leads, read a few in depth, answer one or two and throw the rest out.

If you don't feel guilty for not reading every word in the newspaper, you shouldn't feel guilty about not reading every lead.

It should take you less than 30 minutes to manage your leads account each day: Skim leads and write responses in 10 minutes. No more than that. If you spend more than 10 minutes writing a message, you are doing something wrong. The system is easy. Don't make it difficult.

If you get one good quote a month, you will increase your visibility exponentially each year.

Stick with the system. It works!

46.   Re-use Material on Your Blog, Ezine, etc.

There's no wasted time with PR LEADS.

While you won't be quoted every time you submit a response to a reporter, don't think you've wasted your time, either.

You can use that answer in any printed material you have, or on your website, your newsletter, your Ezine, your speeches or your next book.

When you write your responses, you are actually creating content that can help impress your clients and prospects.

Make the most of your knowledge.

47.   Send Old Tips to Similar Leads

You might have noticed that many reporters write the same kinds of stories and ask the same questions over and over again!

There is nothing new under the sun.

For example, you'll always see leads on:
- How to lose weight

- How to improve your love life

- How to have happier, healthier kids

- How to get ahead on your job

- Thanksgiving ideas

- Christmas ideas

- Back to school fashions

- Leadership tips

- Sales tips

You'll notice patterns as well.

You'll save a lot of time responding when you use your classic answers.

It would be a good idea to save your tips and re-use them when appropriate.

48.   File Your Responses

Keep a copy of your response and the original lead.

When a reporter calls you several weeks later, you might not remember the lead, or what you wrote. If you keep a copy of both messages, you can refresh your memory quickly.

Here's what to do.

At the bottom of your response to reporters, paste the original message.

When you need to find the message, use your email program to search for the reporter's name. It should display quickly!

You can even create a new folder in your email program and label it "Publicity Leads." Place all your correspondence with reporters there so you can find it easily.

49.   Get Experts for Your Articles and Books

Do you need to quote experts in your articles, blogs and books?

You can submit queries just like reporters do!

Simply go to your account on ProfNet and post a message under the tab labeled "Create Member Inquiry." Your message will go out to experts who can help! This is an included feature of your PR LEADS service.

This can be a great help to you when you are writing articles and books and need to find an expert to quote. A number of clients do this already, so I thought you'd want to know about it as well.

It's easy, it's fast and it is free!

50.   How to Find Your Articles and Quotes

How will I know if reporters quote me, or use my material?

Hardly any reporters will send you copies of articles. They just don't have the time.

Many reporters will send you an email asking for permission to use your material, or will send you an email asking you additional questions or to set a time to talk on the phone. When this happens, ASK THEM when the article will appear.

Write that info on your calendar. When that day arrives, check the website of that publication. Yes, even print publications post most articles on their website, so you don't have to fly to Dallas to get a copy of the Morning News!

51.   Find Your Quotes with Google Alerts

You can also use a free clipping service that Google offers: http://www.Google.com/alerts

You'll fill out a simple form that asks for your name, email address, search terms and how often you want to be notified. It is simple!

You can tell Google to look for your name, or your book title, even your URL. Google will send you an email whenever they find something new!

It's free. Try it now so you can see your articles!

Please note, Google can't find everything, so you might be seeing just a portion of your articles. It's a great first start!

Many of my clients have found articles this way. Of course, you can go to Google and type your name for articles in the past, but Google Alerts will do this for you automatically for the future.

52.   Manage Your Phone Image

Does your answering machine present the professional image you need?

Do reporters hear messages suitable for a family, but not a best-selling author or business consultant?

Do they hear kids in the background, or static and electronic noises?

If they do, you might lose the interview.

How can you tell?

Call yourself -- and listen critically for anything that can damage your reputation.

53.   Check Your Caller ID

Reporters can see who is calling before they answer the phone. Your caller ID appears the instant the phone starts ringing.

Does your caller ID position you properly? Does it have your name or a business name? That's fine.

Do you block your caller ID? Reporters might think you are a telemarketing company.

Not sure what it says? Call a friend and ask her what the message reads.

You might be very surprised!

Section 3: What Do You Do With Publicity?

While many people get publicity, they do not know what to do with it.

Remember the old saying, "If a tree falls in the forest and no one is there, does it make any noise?"

The same is true with publicity. You can't expect every one of your prospects to find your article in a newspaper or on a blog. You must tell the world that you've been quoted.

This section will show you easy ways to trumpet your success so you can get more prospects and more business.

54.   Build Your Business with Your Quotes

Here are ways to leverage your publicity

1.   Send the link to the article via email to current clients.

2.   Send the link to the article via email to former clients.

3.   Send the link to the article via email to prospects.

4.   Post reprints on your website.

5.   Frame them in your office.

6.   Include articles in book proposals.

7.   Include articles in new business proposals.

8.   Include articles in new business PowerPoint presentations.

9.   Mention articles in your blog.

10.   Mention articles in your newsletter.

11.   Mention articles on the front page of your website.

12.   Send print copies to your current clients.

13.   Send print copies to your former clients.

14.   Send print copies to your prospects.

15.   Mention your articles in your website bio.

16.   Mention your articles in your speech introduction.

17.   Create a list of all the articles you were quoted in and post it to your website's "newsroom' section.

You don't have to do all these steps. If you do only ONE of these steps, you will be doing more than you are now to build your business. Take action today to build your business with publicity!

55.   Tweet Your Publicity

Post notices of your articles on Twitter, LinkedIn, Facebook, Google+ and any other social media your clients and prospects use.

56.   Re-Print Articles on Your Web Site

Many publications make serious money by selling reprint rights.

You should also be aware of the copyright laws:

1. You cannot print the article in full on your site, nor can you print their logo, unless you have permission.

2. You can link to the article on the publication's web site. You don't have to ask permission.

3. You can use 2-3 sentences from the article without permission (e.g. USA TODAY calls Dan Janal "a true cyberspace marketing pioneer" which they in fact, did write.)

If the article can really help you build your business, then you might want to bite the bullet and pay the big bucks. Consider it advertising.

57.   Working with Publicists

We all know that book publicists and publishing companies rarely give you the time of day after your book has been out for 30 days.

One of our PR LEADERS gets more respect -- and work -- from her publicist by following a simple tip:

When you get publicity, tell her! She'll be your best friend.

Why?

Because, you are making her look good.

She will put the clip or clips in her monthly report to her bosses. They'll think she's doing a great job. She will turn around and help you when she can -- if she is smart!

58.   Press Releases Can Help Get Publicity

Press releases can be a great way to get your message to reporters and prospects -- and build your search engine rankings as well.

I issued a press release and had amazing results -- and you can too.

It appeared on Forbes.com, Hoovers.com, and three dozen city business journals -- amazing!

Read my story here:

http://www.prleads.com/blog/heres-a-press-release-distribution-service-thats-low-cost-and-highly-effective/

If you don't know how to write a press release, or if you don't know what to put into a press release, don't worry. We will work with you to create a press release that delivers results.

For info, go to http://www.PressReleaseSender.com or call me at 952-380-1554.

59. Create a Wall of Fame with Your Articles

Frame the best articles and hang them on the walls.

Your clients will be very impressed to see your Wall of Fame!

They will be more likely to refer you to their friends, schedule repeat visits and take your advice!

You might want to do this if you work out of your home. You'll see the articles and that will make you feel good about yourself and it will inspire you to keep on getting publicity.

60.   Post Your Responses to Your Blog

After a reporter has interviewed you, you can tell your blog readers and newsletter readers:

"I was interviewed by Newspaper A and here's what I told them."

Then print the tip you offered.

There's not wasted time with PR LEADS. When you create content and post it to your blog or Ezine, you are a winner in the eyes of your readers and clients.

61.   Celebrate Your Success!

Tell the world about the PR that you are getting. Look at how Kevin Donlin, author of "Guerilla Marketing for Job Hunters" shows his publicity on the front page of his site:

http://www.gm4jh.com/

62.   Use Publicity to Boost Search Engine Rankings

Many people on the Internet find new books, consultants and speakers by searching Google.

You have probably tried a few ways to improve your rankings on Google, if you are like most people.

You might have asked your friends to link to your site.

But did you know that not all links are created equal? Google has assigned a "page rank" or "PR" (that's right) to many sites. The better the page rank, the more Google values the link to your site.

If you get a link to your site from a newspaper or magazine, Google will think your site rocks.

So keep plugging away at publicity. You'll improve your search engine rankings so more people will find you - long after the newspaper is old news!

63.   Additional Tips from Dan Janal

I post messages on my blog several times a week. Would you like to get my blog? It is simple. Go to:

> http://www.prleads.com/blog

Put your email address into the box or sign up for the RSS feed.

I answer questions on my blog all the time. You can send questions to me at dan@prleads.com.

You can also follow me on social media:

> Twitter: @prleads
>
> Facebook: http://www.facebook.com/prleads
>
> LinkedIn: Dan Janal
>
> Google+: PRLEADS

Section 4: Success Stories

You might be wondering what the value of publicity is.

Publicity can help build healthy businesses in many ways:

1. Increase your visibility.

2. Increase your credibility.

3. Gives you credibility to raise your speaking fees.

4. Gives you credibility to raise your consulting fees.

5. Proves to book editors that you are an effective marketer (which can result in larger advances for your books).

6. Makes you easier to find on Google.

7. Helps you stand apart from your competitors.

8. Advertises your business and products without spending a penny on ads.

This section shows a few examples of clients who have turned publicity into money. For more examples, go to http://www.prleads.com and look for testimonials and case studies.

64. PR LEADS Helps Speaker Double His Fees!

Patrick Snow was quoted on the front page of the USA TODAY and two things changed right away.

1. He doubled his speaking fee.

2. Meeting planners didn't negotiate his fee any longer. They figured, if he was on the front page of USA TODAY, he was worth that fee!

Patrick is just like you, a good person with a great message. But when he got big publicity, he found the leverage he needed to raise and justify his fees.

Isn't it time you raised your rates?

That's another way that PR LEADS can help you make money!

65.   PR LEADS Helps Author Get Bigger Book Advance

Psychologist Larina Kase tells us that when she wrote her book proposal, she included articles in which PR LEADS helped her get quoted.

The result: a book advance that was twice the average of her peers! Congratulations, Larina!

Be sure to tell your literary agent and acquisition authors that you use PR LEADS. They'll treat you with added professional respect when you do.

That's another way that PR LEADS can help you make more money!

66. PR LEADS Helps Relationship Coach
Tina Tessina Gets Speaking Engagement and a Paid Column in Top Magazine

Psychologist and author Tina Tessina obtained a major speaking contract and a paid series of columns in a major women's magazine as a result of using the publicity service and getting massive amounts of media coverage.

"I regard PR LEADS as the single most effective PR tool I've used. I've been quoted in the NY Times and everywhere else, gotten clients, paid speaking opportunities and promoted my books, all with leads from PR LEADS. They're the best quality leads available," said Tina Tessina, a Los Angeles based psychotherapist and bestselling author of more than 13 books. Her website is http://www.TinaTessina.com

"Many consultants, coaches and thought leaders have used PR LEADS to get publicity that helped them get speaking engagements, justify their fees and even raise their fees," said Dan Janal, president of PR LEADS (www.prleads.com) and an acknowledged publicity expert and publicity speaker.

"Publicity helps experts and speakers in several ways. First, the articles bring your name and topic to the attention of meeting planners, speakers bureaus and decision makers at companies and associations who are always looking for the next big thing," said Janal, who has spoken at conferences all around the world – literally from Beijing to Budapest. He has also written six books on Internet Publicity and Internet Marketing that have been translated into six languages.

"Speakers can stand out from the crowd when they use publicity. They should always include their publicity on their web sites and in their speaker kits to help convince meeting planners to hire them," said Janal, who offers publicity coaching for speakers.

67. PR LEADS Helps Boston Consultant
Leadership Consultant Gets Book Publishing Contract

Leadership consultant Stephen R. Balzac obtained a book contract as a result of using the publicity service and getting massive amounts of media coverage.

"Without a doubt I landed a book contract for 'The 36-Hour Course in Organizational Development' from McGraw-Hill thanks to PR Leads," said Stephen R. Balzac, President, 7 Steps Ahead, LLC. *"I've lost track of the number of times I've been quoted."*

"Many consultants, coaches and thought leaders have used PR LEADS to get publicity that helped them get contracts from the biggest and best publishers," said Dan Janal, president of PR LEADS (www.prleads.com).

"Publicity helps authors in several ways. First, the articles bring your name and topic to the attention of publishing editors who are always looking for the next big thing," said Janal, who has written six books on Internet Publicity and Internet Marketing that have been translated into six languages.

68.   Lingerie Company Increases Sales by 65%
Thanks to Publicity from PR LEADS

Lingerie Website JadaMichaels.com achieved a 65% increase in sales after MSNMoney.com wrote about the company. The reporter learned about the boutique lingerie company by posting a query on PR LEADS.com the most effective reporter-to-source publicity leads referral company.

"We had more than 11,000 hits in one day," said Jada Michaels, president of JadaMichaels.com, whose motto is "Make Life Sexy™" The company sells lingerie for every shape and size. *"I can't believe how much one good write up does. It has actually now opened the door to another great article as the original journalist referred me onto a successful colleague."*

"PR LEADS has helped many small businesses sell products and services," said Dan Janal, president of PR LEADS.com. *"We get hundreds of requests from reporters who need to find sources for their articles and they trust us to share their messages with only the best and brightest authors, thought leaders, industry experts and innovative small businesses."*

Based in Chicago, Jada Michaels.com offers a contemporary lingerie collection for women of all sizes. Jada Michaels has a passion for trendy designs, impeccable craftsmanship, bold colors, and eye-catching prints with luscious fabrics and flirty details. The line features lingerie for women of all sizes including the Baby Got Curves collection for plus-size women. The holiday collection is an ode to Hollywood's golden era. The collection has been featured in national magazines, such as People, Maxim, InStyle, and Cosmo, while celebrity fans include Katy Perry, Kim Kardashian and Denise Richards.

69.   Intuition Author Credits PR LEADS
Lands New Book Contract

Intuition author Lynn Robinson credited the PR LEADS publicity service with helping her get a book contract.

"I just signed a contract with Jossey Bass (a division of Wiley & Sons) to revise and update my first book, 'Divine Intuition: Your Guide to Creating a Life You Love.' The fact that I'd received so much media attention was one of the factors that sealed the deal!" she said. The book will be in bookstores in late 2012. Her current books, including "Listen" and "Trust Your Gut" are available on her website and at Amazon.com.

"Intuition is a gift from the Universe — from God, if you will — that will guide us unerringly to the realization of our hopes and dreams," says Robinson, author of this uncommonly readable book. Using personal experience, beautiful illustrations, inspiring quotes, simple exercises, and stories from thousands of clients, Robinson demonstrates that intuition is a gift from the Universe that anyone can cultivate as an unwavering and reliable source of wisdom and guidance.

Lynn A. Robinson, M.Ed., is one of the nation's leading experts on the topic of intuition. She's a popular and widely recognized author and motivational speaker who works with businesses and individuals as an intuitive advisor, offering insights into goals, decisions and strategies. Clients usually call her when they're in the midst of change and transition.

Lynn has been recognized by Boston Magazine, where she was voted "Best Intuitive" by readers and editors.

Section 5: Taking the Next Step

You'll need tools to take your publicity to the next level. We've negotiated discounts on many publicity services from industry leading companies, like PR Newswire, to help save you money on press release distribution, media databases and other services.

We also provide publicity coaching and consulting, as well as writing press releases and pitch letters. Please review this section for ideas and contact us at 952-380-9844 or www.PRLEADSPLUS.com for information on all our services.

Good luck!

70.   Recommended Publicity and Marketing Services

PR LEADS – Get queries from reporters at the top media.
Only $99 a month
> **http://www.PRLEADS.com**

PR LEADS PLUS Press Release Services – Send press releases
to reporters via PR Newswire for guaranteed placement and results
to build your brand. Three levels of service – from complete done
for you to do-it-yourself.
> **http://www.PressReleaseSender.com**

71.   Speaker Match Shows How to Get Speaking Gigs

Imagine PR LEADS for speakers. Instead of getting leads from
reporters who want to find sources, you could get leads from
meeting planners who want to hire speakers.
You need to explore SpeakerMatch.
http://www.marketerschoice.com/app/aftrack.asp?AFID=79780

72.   Media Databases Help You Find Reporters to Pitch

Would you be interested in taking your business to the next level by contacting the media directly?

We have the most up-to-date media lists with more than 500,000 contacts at newspapers, magazines, radio stations and television stations.

Now you can send your messages directly to media who could write about you and your services.

Each list comes with:

> Name
> Email
> Phone
> Address
> Topics
> Personal notes
> Website
> Circulation
> Media type
> And much, much more

This is a great way to contact reporters at newspapers, magazines, TV and radio!

It's a great investment in your business and it is very affordable.

You can get a highly targeted list for just $197.

For details, see http://www.BullsEyePublicity.com
> or email susan@prleads.com
> or call us at 952-380-9844, we will show you how it works.

## 73.	Do You Need a PR Coach to Get More Publicity?

If you need a PR coach or consultant, let's see if I am the right person to help you.

To arrange for a complimentary 20-minute introduction session to see if coaching or consulting can help you reach your goals,
go to http://www.PublicityLeadstoProfits
or email me dan@prleads.com.

74.   About the Author – Dan Janal

Dan Janal is president and founder of PRLEADS PLUS.com, a public relations service that helps authors, speakers, coaches, consultants and small businesses get more visibility and credibility so they can sell more products with greater ease.

USA Today called Dan Janal "a true cyberspace marketing pioneer" because he wrote one of the first books ever written about Internet marketing way back in 1994.

Dan is known for his pioneering work in online public relations through his books, speeches coaching. His clients have been featured in nearly every major newspaper and magazine.

Dan has lectured everywhere from Beijing to Budapest, as well as across the U.S., Canada, Mexico and Brazil. He's even taught at Berkeley and Stanford.

Dan has written six books for John Wiley & Sons and those books have been translated into six languages. Dan believes that publicity and marketing should be about getting results.

A former award-winning newspaper reporter and editor, Dan interviewed President Gerald Ford and First Lady Barbara Bush.

Discover more about Dan's publicity and coaching services at:

http://www.PRLEADSplus.com

75.   Book Dan Janal to Speak at Your Conference

Does your company, organization or association need to learn the latest trends in online marketing and publicity?

I am an inspiring and entertaining speaker who can move your audiences to enlightenment and to take action.

Keynote Speeches:
- New trends in online marketing
- How to make the Internet work for you

Breakout Sessions
- How to write press releases that are read and make money
- How to rank high in the search engines with publicity
- How to leverage your publicity to fame and fortune

For more information go to http://www.janal.com

GoldStars Speakers Bureau represents Dan.

Contact Andrea Gold at andrea@goldstars.com.